CONTENTS

The Stoic Woman: Finding Inner Strength to Live a Fulfilling Life

"Discover the Principles of Stoicism to Cultivate Self-Discipline, Resilience, and Happiness in the Modern Era"

Susanna Blumen

"The true greatness of a woman lies in her ability to maintain serenity and strength amidst the tribulations of life. As the famous Stoic philosopher Seneca once said, 'It is not because things are difficult that we do not dare, it is because we do not dare that they are difficult.' Let us draw inspiration from Stoic wisdom to face every obstacle with determination, finding within ourselves the inner strength necessary to overcome any adversity. Let us remember that we are the architects of our own happiness, capable of shaping our minds, characters, and actions in accordance with reason and virtue. May each day serve as a reminder of our power to transform our lives and leave a positive mark on the world. May our pursuit of Stoic wisdom lead us to live a fulfilling, authentic, and meaningful life, transcending the limitations imposed by society and finding peace in our own existence. Let us wake up each morning with the purpose of becoming the best version of ourselves and courageously embrace the Stoic path to feminine greatness!"

1. INTRODUCTION

"Suffering arises from resistance to change." - Marcus Aurelius

In this chapter, we will dive into the fascinating world of Stoicism and its relationship with women in today's society. Before delving into the specific points we will address, it is important to establish an introduction that situates us in the appropriate context.

Stoicism is an ancient philosophy that has left a profound mark on history and has influenced the way people face life's challenges. Throughout the centuries, many women have embraced Stoic principles and found invaluable guidance in navigating the ups and downs of existence.

In this chapter, we will explore what Stoicism is, its philosophical foundations, and how Stoic women manifested themselves in ancient times. Through examples of notable women who practiced Stoicism, we will discover how these women found strength, resilience, and wisdom amidst adversity.

Furthermore, we will analyze why Stoicism is relevant for women in the modern era. In a world that presents unique challenges and constantly evolving expectations, women can find in Stoicism a practical and empowering approach to confronting obstacles and developing a resilient mindset.

As we delve into this chapter, we invite readers to explore their own connection to Stoicism and discover how these principles can enrich their lives and provide them with a renewed perspective on the power of their own inner strength.

WHAT IS STOICISM?

Stoicism is a philosophical school that originated in ancient Greece during the Hellenistic period, around the 3rd century BCE. It was founded by Zeno of Citium, who taught in Athens from 301 BCE until his death in 262 BCE. Zeno taught at the Stoa Poikile, a painted colonnade near the marketplace in Athens, hence the name Stoicism.

The Stoic philosophy centered around the idea that virtue is the only good thing and that the good life is one lived in accordance with reason and nature. For Stoics, reason is the most important human faculty, and nature is the principle that governs everything that exists.

Stoics also believed in the idea that the universe is a coherent and rational whole, and that everything that happens within it is destined to happen. Therefore, accepting events and circumstances as they arise and living in accordance with nature are fundamental to achieving happiness.

Notable Stoics include Seneca, Epictetus, and Marcus Aurelius, who lived in different times and places but shared the same philosophy. Seneca was a renowned philosopher, writer, and Roman senator who lived in the 1st century CE and became the tutor of Emperor Nero. Epictetus was a Stoic philosopher born in Phrygia, present-day Turkey, in the 1st century CE and was a former slave before becoming a philosopher. Marcus Aurelius was the last of the Five Good Emperors of Rome, ruling from 161 to 180 CE.

The Stoic philosophy spread from ancient Greece to Rome and beyond, and was adopted by many philosophers, writers, and political leaders. Stoics believed that philosophy was a practical guide to life, and that the good life is achieved through the cultivation of virtue and reason, the acceptance of what cannot be controlled, and living in harmony with nature.

In the modern era, Stoicism has experienced a resurgence of interest, particularly in the fields of business, psychology, and self-help. Many find in Stoic philosophy a valuable tool for dealing with stress, uncertainty, and the challenges of modern life.

STOIC WOMEN IN ANCIENT TIMES

During ancient times, Stoicism was a philosophy practiced by both men and women. While most historical records focus on notable Stoic men, there were also Stoic women who influenced philosophy and society at large.

One of the earliest and most notable examples of a Stoic woman was Antigone, who lived in Athens in the 3rd century BCE. She was known for her wisdom and virtue, and it is said that she taught philosophy to her husband. She is also said to have maintained a Stoic attitude and stoically accepted the death of her children.

Another notable Stoic woman was Cornelia Africana, the mother of the Gracchi brothers in 2nd century BCE Rome. She was known as a wise and intelligent woman who educated her children with Stoic principles. It is also believed that she maintained a Stoic attitude when her husband died.

Although Stoicism was not a common philosophy for women in antiquity, those who practiced it were not necessarily seen as rare. The central idea of Stoicism, accepting fate and finding inner peace through virtue, was valued for both men and women.

However, it is worth noting that Stoic women often faced challenges in a society that was based on gender inequality. Women were expected to focus on their roles as wives and mothers, and philosophy was seen as a pastime for men. Nevertheless, Stoic women persevered and found ways to practice their philosophy in a world that underestimated them.

In summary, while Stoicism was a philosophy mainly practiced by men in antiquity, there were also notable Stoic women who influenced philosophy and society. Although women practicing Stoicism faced challenges in a society that undervalued their role, they persevered and found ways to practice their philosophy and live according to their principles.

WHY IS STOICISM RELEVANT FOR WOMEN IN THE MODERN ERA?

Stoicism is a philosophy that focuses on the importance of ethics, virtue, and reason as guides for living a fulfilling and happy life. These values are equally relevant for men and women, and in fact, in antiquity, many women adopted and practiced Stoicism with great success.

In the modern era, Stoicism remains relevant for women for several reasons. Firstly, Stoicism teaches us to focus on what we can control and let go of concerns that are beyond our control. This can be especially helpful for women who often face challenges and obstacles beyond their control, such as discrimination, gender-based violence, or the gender pay gap. By focusing on what we can control, we can find ways to overcome these obstacles and live a fulfilling and happy life.

Secondly, Stoicism teaches us to be resilient and face life's challenges with courage and determination. Women have historically been marginalized and discriminated against in many areas of society, and Stoicism can help women develop the strength and perseverance needed to overcome these obstacles and fight for equality and justice.

Additionally, Stoicism emphasizes the importance of wisdom, justice, and moderation, which can help women develop a more balanced and fair perspective on the world and themselves. Women often face social and cultural pressures to be perfect, attractive, and accommodating, and Stoicism can help counteract these unrealistic expectations and allow them to live according to their own values and beliefs.

In summary, Stoicism is relevant for women in the modern era because it helps us focus on what we can control, be resilient in the face of adversity, and develop a more balanced and fair perspective on the world.

2. THE STOIC PRINCIPLES FOR A FULFILLING LIFE

"A fulfilling life lies in the serenity of the Stoic mind."

S toicism offers a practical and useful philosophy for a fulfilling and satisfying life. In this section, we will explore how Stoic principles can be applied in the daily lives of women to achieve a fulfilling life. From the importance of cultivating resilience to the value of focusing on what can be controlled and learning to live in the present moment, we will discover how these teachings can be helpful in everyday situations such as work, school, family life, and relationships. Through this approach, women can find greater inner strength and the ability to face life's challenges.

LIVING IN ACCORDANCE WITH REASON

Living in accordance with reason is one of the fundamental principles of Stoicism. Instead of following impulses and emotions, it is about acting in a reasoned and conscious manner. This approach can be particularly relevant for women in the modern era, as they often face challenges and pressures in different areas of life.

Acting in accordance with reason involves making more careful and conscious decisions that take into account long-term consequences and core values. For example, if a woman has to make an important career decision, such as accepting or declining a new job, acting in accordance with reason would involve carefully considering all relevant factors, such as job satisfaction, salary, growth opportunities, location, and impact on personal life.

There are many benefits to living in accordance with reason, both on an individual and collective level. Firstly, it helps us make more informed and conscious decisions that allow us to move in the direction we desire. Secondly, it enables us to take control of our emotions and not be dominated by them. It also helps us to be more considerate of others and our environment, as we carefully consider how our actions will affect those around us.

PRACTICING SELF-DISCIPLINE

Practicing self-discipline is a fundamental aspect of Stoicism that can be highly beneficial for women in modern life. Self-discipline refers to the ability to control one's own actions, thoughts, and emotions to achieve a desired long-term goal.

Self-discipline can be challenging to implement and maintain as it may require short-term sacrifices and constant effort to stay motivated. However, the long-term benefits are invaluable, especially for women seeking to improve their lives and achieve their goals.

Self-discipline can help you develop healthy habits such as regular exercise, eating well, getting enough sleep, and reducing stress. These habits are important for a healthy and happy life.

Furthermore, self-discipline can help you overcome challenges and obstacles that arise on your path to success. Instead of giving up at the first difficulty, self-discipline allows you to stay focused on your goal and work to overcome any obstacle.

Maintaining self-discipline can be difficult, especially when facing distractions or temptations. However, consistent practice and perseverance can help you develop this crucial skill.

For example, you can start with small actions, such as setting a study or work schedule and consistently sticking to it daily. Another approach is to set realistic and achievable short-term goals so that you can maintain motivation and track your progress.

A practical example in daily life could be a woman who wants to lose weight. To achieve her goal, she can establish an exercise routine and plan healthy meals. Additionally, she can set small short-term goals, such as losing half a kilogram per week, to stay motivated and monitor her progress. With perseverance and self-discipline, she can achieve her goal and improve her overall health and well-being.

In summary, practicing self-discipline is essential to achieving your goals and improving your life overall. Although it can be challenging, the long-term benefits are invaluable, especially for women in the modern era seeking to enhance their lives and achieve success.

CULTIVATING RESILIENCE

Resilience is the ability of a person to face and overcome adverse and challenging situations while maintaining a positive attitude and a solution-oriented perspective. The term originated in psychology and refers to the capacity of individuals to recover after experiencing trauma or intense stress.

Resilience is particularly relevant for women in the modern era due to the multiple challenges they face in their daily lives, such as gender discrimination, harassment, domestic violence, and the gender pay gap. By developing resilience, women can enhance their ability to confront and successfully overcome these challenges.

Moreover, resilience can have numerous benefits for women's mental and physical health. By cultivating resilience, they can reduce their stress levels, improve self-esteem, and develop a more positive outlook on life. They can also build a greater capacity to cope with anxiety and depression.

However, being resilient can sometimes be difficult. Women may feel overwhelmed by the stress and pressure of modern life's demands, which can hinder their resilience. Additionally, there may be cultural barriers that impede resilience development, such as the belief that women should naturally be strong and resilient without needing to work on it.

An example of how women can cultivate resilience in their daily lives is through the practice of mindfulness. Meditation and yoga are techniques that can help women develop awareness and mindfulness in the present moment, thereby enhancing their ability to face challenging situations. Additionally, creating an emotional and social support network can also be an effective way to develop resilience, as it can provide a safe space to talk and receive support during times of stress and adversity.

FOCUSING ON WHAT CAN BE CONTROLLED

Focusing on what can be controlled is one of the fundamental principles of Stoicism. It involves directing our attention to those things we can control rather than those that are beyond our power. To better understand this concept, it's important to define what we mean by control. Control refers to our ability to act and make decisions in relation to something, whether it's in our personal or professional life.

It's important to recognize that there are many things in our lives that are outside of our control, such as the weather, the global economy, or the actions of others. If we focus on trying to control these things, we will only experience frustration, anxiety, and stress. Instead, by focusing on what we can control, we give ourselves the opportunity to act more effectively and feel more secure.

In many situations, it's easy to lose control of our emotions, especially in circumstances that personally affect us. For example, a woman may lose control if her partner cheats on her or if her boss treats her unfairly. However, it's important to remember that while we can't control the actions of others, we can control our response to them. The ability to stay calm and emotionally balanced in difficult situations is a valuable skill that allows us to make more informed decisions.

Cultivating the ability to focus on what we can control helps us make better decisions and avoid the anxiety and stress that come from trying to control what is beyond our grasp. Of course, this doesn't mean we should give up on our goals or aspirations. It simply means that we should direct our energy towards the actions we can control and trust that the rest will resolve itself.

An everyday life example could be a woman who is job hunting. If she focuses on sending applications to companies that are clearly out of her reach or not hiring at the moment, she will be wasting her time and efforts. On the other hand, if she focuses on researching companies that have job opportunities available and sends applications to those companies, she will have a higher chance of finding employment. This way, she will be directing her energy and efforts towards what she can control, rather than what is beyond her reach.

LIVING IN THE PRESENT MOMENT

Living in the present moment is an idea derived from stoicism that invites us to focus on the present instead of worrying about the future or regretting the past. Rather than dwelling on what has already happened or what is yet to come, we center ourselves in the here and now.

To live in the present moment, it is important to practice mindfulness. This means being aware of our thoughts, emotions, physical sensations, and the environment around us. When we are mindful of the present moment, we can savor the small things in life and find meaning in each moment.

Women, in particular, can greatly benefit from living in the present moment. In our current society, many women feel overwhelmed by multiple responsibilities, including work, family, household chores, and social obligations. The idea of living in the present may seem challenging to achieve, but it can actually help us find balance and reduce stress.

Moreover, living in the present moment allows us to be more aware of our emotions and reactions. We can learn to recognize negative thinking patterns and replace them with more positive and constructive thoughts.

A practical example of living in the present moment is dedicating daily time to do something we enjoy and that allows us to be fully present. It can be anything from taking a nature walk to reading a book, cooking, or spending time with friends and family. During that time, try not to think about anything else but the activity you are engaged in, focusing on the details and fully enjoying the moment.

3. PRACTICAL APPLICATION OF STOICISM IN DAILY LIFE

"Happiness depends upon ourselves." - Seneca

In today's world, many women face various challenges in their daily lives, from work and family to personal relationships and mental health. In this regard, stoicism can be a useful tool to help women find inner strength to confront these challenges and stay focused on what truly matters.

The practical application of stoicism in daily life involves incorporating stoic principles into everyday situations to find the mental clarity and inner peace necessary to navigate life's ups and downs. From a woman's perspective, this may involve developing skills of self-determination and independence, cultivating resilience in the face of adversity, and establishing healthy and fulfilling relationships.

In this section, we will explore how women can apply stoic principles in their daily lives to find the inner strength necessary to overcome challenges and achieve their goals. Through practical examples and helpful advice, we hope to provide valuable guidance for women seeking a more fulfilling and satisfying life through stoicism.

APPLYING STOIC PRINCIPLES IN EVERYDAY SITUATIONS

Stoicism is not just a theoretical philosophy but also a daily practice that can help us navigate difficult situations. Here are some practical examples of how to apply Stoic principles in everyday situations, with a focus on women:

1. Living in accordance with reason:

- Instead of being driven by emotions, we can make rational and thoughtful decisions in conflict situations. For instance, if someone insults us, rather than impulsively and violently responding, we can think about how to respond rationally and constructively to resolve the issue.
- Instead of excessive worry about the future, we can focus on the present and on things within our control. For example, if we're concerned about our future work, we can concentrate on doing our current job to the best of our ability and seek opportunities for growth and improvement.

2. Practicing self-discipline:

- We can establish healthy habits, such as exercising regularly, eating a balanced diet, and getting enough sleep, even when we don't feel like it. For example, if we feel tired after work, we can motivate ourselves to engage in a brief workout to stay active and healthy.
- We can resist the temptation to consume drugs or alcohol excessively or spend our money on unnecessary things. For instance, if we're tempted to buy an expensive item we don't need, we can remember our commitment to self-discipline and resist the temptation.

3. Cultivating resilience:

- We can learn to see difficult situations as opportunities for growth and improvement instead of getting discouraged by obstacles. For example, if we have been laid off from our job, we can seek ways to enhance our skills and education to find better employment in the future.

- We can learn to effectively manage stress and anxiety through relaxation techniques, meditation, or therapy. For instance, if we feel overwhelmed by work-related stress, we can take time to meditate or practice yoga to regain calmness and mental clarity.

4. Focusing on what is within our control:

- We can stop worrying about things that are beyond our control, such as other people's behaviour or external events. For example, if someone treats us poorly, we can accept that we cannot control their behaviour and focus on our own actions and reactions.

- We can learn to make conscious and responsible decisions instead of being driven by external circumstances. For instance, if we encounter a problem at work, we can evaluate our options and make decisions based on our own ethics and values.

Overall, applying Stoic principles in everyday situations can help us become more mindful and reflective in our actions, face difficult situations calmly, and cultivate a positive and proactive attitude toward life's challenges.

THE IMPORTANCE OF MEDITATION
AND REFLECTION IN STOICISM

In Stoicism, meditation and reflection are key tools for achieving self-discipline, resilience, and focusing on what can be controlled. Through meditation and reflection, Stoics sought to find tranquility and wisdom, as well as to face life's challenges with a clear and focused mind.

There are several types of meditation that can be practiced in Stoicism, such as mindfulness meditation, visualisation meditation, and meditation on death. Mindfulness meditation focuses on being fully present in the current moment, without judgment or distractions. Visualisation meditation involves imagining a desired situation or outcome and focusing on it in a positive way. Meditation on death, on the other hand, is a practice that helps Stoics confront death with serenity and value life more.

On the other hand, reflection in Stoicism involves asking profound questions and contemplating the nature of life, morality, and virtue. It also involves examining one's own thoughts and actions, as well as learning from past experiences to improve in the present. Reflection can be carried out in various forms, such as writing in a journal or silently asking fundamental questions.

Meditation and reflection are important in Stoicism because they help practitioners develop a calm and focused mind, find wisdom, and face life's challenges with a broader perspective. They also help cultivate self-discipline and resilience by promoting greater awareness and control of one's own thoughts and emotions.

An example of meditation and reflection in everyday life can be taking a few minutes each day to sit in silence and focus on the breath, allowing thoughts to come and go without judgment. Another practice could be dedicating time each evening to reflect on the day's experiences and how they could have been handled more effectively.

In summary, meditation and reflection are fundamental practices in Stoicism that help develop a calm and focused mind, cultivate self-discipline and resilience, and face life's challenges with wisdom and perspective.

HOW TO DEVELOP A STOIC ATTITUDE IN WORK, SCHOOL, AND FAMILY LIFE

In daily life, women face various challenges in work, school, and family life, which can lead to stress, anxiety, and frustration. However, by adopting a stoic attitude, they can learn to deal with these challenges more effectively and build a more fulfilling life. In this regard, Stoicism can be particularly beneficial for women due to its principles of self-control, perseverance, and equanimity.

By adopting a stoic attitude in work, school, and family life, women can benefit from increased ability to handle difficult situations, greater resilience, and enhanced focus on long-term goals. Additionally, Stoicism can also help women maintain control over their emotions, enabling them to make clearer and more effective decisions.

While adopting a stoic attitude can be beneficial, it can also pose challenges. Some women may feel that they are suppressing their emotions, which can lead to a sense of disconnection. However, the practice of Stoicism is not about repressing emotions but rather about learning to manage them effectively. Moreover, there may be moments when it is difficult to maintain a stoic attitude, especially in highly emotional situations.

Developing a stoic attitude in work, school, and family life is especially relevant for women as they face unique challenges in each of these areas. Here are some practical examples of how to apply stoic principles in each context:

1. At work:

- Focus on what can be controlled: A woman can find empowerment by focusing on her own performance and professional development, rather than worrying about others' perception. She can set realistic goals and work diligently to achieve them, recognizing that success is not solely determined by external factors such as promotion or recognition.

- Practice acceptance: In a workplace, unfair or challenging situations may arise. A stoic woman can accept that she will not always have control over others' decisions or circumstances and instead focus on how to respond constructively. For example, instead of resenting an undesirable assignment, she can adopt a learning attitude and seek opportunities to grow and develop.

2. In school:

- Cultivate resilience: Women face academic pressures, competition, and performance expectations. A stoic student can develop resilience by acknowledging that failure and challenges are part of the learning process. She can use obstacles as opportunities to grow, learn from mistakes, and persevere in her pursuit of knowledge.

- Live in the present moment: Instead of constantly worrying about the future or comparing oneself to others, a stoic woman can focus on the present and make the most of each learning experience. This involves mindfully paying attention in classes, actively participating in discussions, and seeking a healthy balance between studying and self-care.

3. In family life:

- Appreciate relationships and practice empathy: A stoic woman can focus on cultivating healthy and meaningful relationships with her family. This entails actively listening, showing compassion, and understanding others' perspectives. By practicing empathy, she can strengthen family bonds and foster an environment of mutual support.

- Set healthy boundaries: In family life, it is essential to establish clear and healthy boundaries to ensure balance and personal well-being. A stoic woman can learn to say "no" when necessary and prioritize her own care and self-determination. This involves recognizing that she cannot control others' expectations or actions but can make conscious decisions and respect her own limits.

By applying these stoic principles in work, school, and family life, women can find greater inner peace, empowerment, and resilience to face daily challenges. It is important to remember that the stoic path does not seek to completely eliminate emotions or challenges but rather to develop a mindset and perspective that allows us to confront them in a more constructive and fulfilling manner.

4. STOICISM AND WOMEN IN CONTEMPORARY SOCIETY

"Stoicism reminds us that a woman's strength lies in her ability to adapt and find her own path in any circumstance."

Stoicism has been a philosophy that has permeated throughout history, both in ancient times and in the present day, and has been applied by people of different genders and social strata. However, we cannot ignore that women have faced and still face certain limitations and discriminations in society, which may give a particular focus to the application of Stoic principles in their case.

In today's society, women continue to face barriers and prejudices in the workplace, family life, and society in general. Stoicism can help women effectively confront these difficulties and develop a resilient attitude in the face of adversity.

One of the main benefits Stoicism can provide to women in modern society is the ability to develop an attitude of empowerment and emotional strength. Instead of allowing external circumstances to dictate their emotions and actions, Stoicism can teach women to take control of their thoughts and emotions, and focus on what is within their control.

Furthermore, Stoicism can be a tool for fostering self-discipline and the ability to make difficult decisions and cope with the consequences. Women can learn to develop the necessary self-discipline to stay focused on their goals and objectives, and to be more resilient in the face of challenges that arise along their path.

Regarding family life, Stoicism can help women develop an attitude of acceptance and find tranquility in stressful or conflict-ridden situations. Instead of allowing negative emotions to take control, women can learn to accept things as they are and find constructive ways to deal with the situations.

In the workplace and academic sphere, Stoicism can be a valuable tool for fostering productivity and leadership skills in women. By focusing on what is within their control and their ability to make informed decisions, women can learn to be effective leaders and make decisions that benefit both themselves and their team or company.

In summary, Stoicism can be a very useful philosophy for women in modern society as it can help them develop an attitude of empowerment, emotional strength, self-discipline, and resilience in the face of adversity. Additionally, it can be a valuable tool for fostering productivity and leadership ability in the workplace and academia, as well as finding tranquility and acceptance in family life.

HOW STOICISM CAN HELP WOMEN FIND INNER STRENGTH TO OVERCOME LIFE'S OBSTACLES

Stoicism can be a powerful tool to help women find the inner strength to overcome life's obstacles. Here are some examples of how Stoic teachings can be applied to everyday situations:

1. Losing a job:

In an increasingly competitive job market, it is common for women to face job loss. Stoicism teaches that we should not cling to material things and should accept the current situation. Instead of worrying about what has been lost, the focus should be on finding a solution and moving forward. A Stoic attitude would allow women to accept the situation calmly and rationally, rather than allowing fear and anxiety to take hold.

2. Caring for a sick family member:

Many women are the primary caregivers for sick family members. The situation can be emotionally and physically draining. Stoicism teaches to focus on what can be controlled and accept what cannot be controlled. Instead of dwelling on the suffering and difficulty of the situation, the woman can focus on actions that can alleviate the burden on the sick family member. Additionally, by accepting that the illness is something beyond her control, she can find greater inner peace.

3. Facing gender discrimination:

Unfortunately, gender discrimination remains a problem in many workplaces and society in general. Women may face sexual harassment, the gender pay gap, and other forms of discrimination

4. Dealing with loss:

Life can be unpredictable, and we often face painful situations such as the loss of a loved one, a breakup, or a job termination, among others. In these situations, Stoicism can help women find the inner strength to overcome these difficult moments. By accepting the reality as it is, women can learn to face loss with serenity and let go of what is no longer there.

5. Managing stress and anxiety:

Modern life can be very stressful and can lead to anxiety and worry. Stoicism can help women deal with stress and anxiety by teaching them to focus on what they can control and accept what they cannot control. Additionally, daily meditation and reflection can help women find inner calmness and reduce stress levels.

6. Overcoming fear:

Fear can be a significant obstacle for many women, whether it's fear of taking risks, fear of failure, or fear of uncertainty. Stoicism can help women overcome these fears and find the inner strength necessary to make brave decisions and move forward in life.

In summary, Stoicism can be a powerful tool for women seeking to find the inner strength necessary to overcome life's obstacles. Through the practice of Stoic philosophy, women can learn to face challenges with courage, maintain calmness in times of crisis, and cultivate a positive perspective in the face of adversity.

THE IMPORTANCE OF SELF-DETERMINATION AND INDEPENDENCE IN STOIC FEMINISM

Stoicism is a philosophy that emphasizes the importance of self-determination and independence, especially for women in contemporary society. Self-determination refers to the ability to make decisions and act in accordance with our own beliefs and values, while independence refers to the ability to be self-sufficient and not rely on anyone else for our happiness and well-being.

In the context of Stoicism, self-determination and independence are fundamental to finding inner peace and lasting happiness. While it may be challenging in a world that bombards us with external expectations and pressures, cultivating self-determination and independence can help us overcome obstacles and achieve our goals.

An example of how self-determination and independence are important in Stoic feminism is when a woman decides to start her own business instead of working for someone else. By making this decision, she is demonstrating her ability to be self-sufficient and take control of her own destiny. While there may be obstacles and difficulties along the way, the fact that she has chosen to pursue her own goals gives her a sense of empowerment and purpose.

Another example is when a woman decides to end a toxic relationship instead of clinging to it out of fear of loneliness. By making this decision, she is demonstrating her ability to be independent and make choices that are better for her emotional and mental well-being. Although it may be challenging at first, the fact that she has made the decision to prioritize her well-being helps her cultivate a stoic attitude and find the inner strength to overcome challenges.

In summary, self-determination and independence are crucial

to Stoic feminism as they allow us to make decisions that are authentic and valuable to ourselves. By developing these qualities, we can cultivate a stoic attitude that helps us find the inner strength to overcome life's obstacles and live according to our own values and beliefs.

How to Cultivate Femininity Without Falling into Stereotypes or Cultural Limitations

Stoicism not only focuses on self-discipline and reason but also on accepting our own nature and respecting others. Therefore, cultivating femininity in Stoicism means recognizing our own strengths and weaknesses as women and working to constantly improve ourselves. This does not mean falling into stereotypes or cultural limitations that prevent us from reaching our full potential. Here are some examples of how to cultivate femininity without falling into stereotypes:

1. Practicing empathy:

Empathy is an important skill to cultivate in anyone, regardless of gender. However, it is often more associated with femininity. Practicing empathy means striving to understand the feelings and perspectives of others, and this can help us build stronger and more meaningful relationships. It can also help us overcome cultural barriers and communicate more effectively with people from different backgrounds.

2. Focusing on personal growth:

Stoicism teaches us to focus on what we can control, and personal growth is one of those things. Instead of worrying about meeting cultural expectations of what it means to be "feminine," we can focus on developing our own skills and strengths. This helps us find a sense of purpose and satisfaction in our lives.

3. Fostering self-determination:

Stoicism emphasizes the importance of owning our own

decisions and actions. Fostering self-determination means taking control of our lives and deciding what is best for us, rather than blindly following what is expected of us. This can include decision-making related to our career, education, relationships, and health.

In summary, cultivating femininity in Stoicism means accepting our own nature as women and working to constantly improve ourselves. This does not mean falling into stereotypes or cultural limitations that prevent us from reaching our full potential. Instead, we can focus on empathy, personal growth, and self-determination to help us find a sense of purpose and satisfaction in our lives.

5. STOICISM AND THE COUPLE

"Applying Stoic principles in a romantic relationship is cultivating a deeper and authentic connection, based on acceptance, empathy, and true love."

I n romantic relationships, women often find themselves dealing with a range of emotions and expectations that can be challenging to handle. Stoicism can be a helpful tool for women seeking to develop a more rational and objective perspective in their relationships. By applying Stoic principles, women can learn to make wiser decisions, become more resilient in the face of adversity, and cultivate healthier and more balanced relationships. In this section, we will explore how women can apply Stoic principles in their romantic relationships and how this can help them find the happiness and emotional stability they seek.

HOW TO APPLY STOIC PRINCIPLES IN A ROMANTIC RELATIONSHIP

Romantic relationships can be an emotional and mental challenge for anyone, and women may face particular challenges. However, applying Stoic principles can help women navigate these difficulties and find peace and happiness in their relationships.

One way women can apply Stoic principles in their romantic relationship is through emotional self-control. Women are often seen as emotional and may struggle to control their feelings in a relationship. However, practicing self-discipline and moderation can help keep emotions in check and avoid overreactions in difficult situations.

Another Stoic principle that women can apply in their romantic relationship is focusing on what they can control. Women often feel the need to change or control their partner to feel secure or happy, but this can be a source of stress and tension in the relationship. Instead, focusing on what they can control in their own lives and accepting their partner as they are can lead to greater peace and happiness.

Finally, mindfulness and reflection are also important for women seeking to apply Stoic principles in their romantic relationship. By taking the time to reflect on their own life and relationships, they can develop a deeper understanding of themselves and their needs and desires in a relationship.

For example, let's imagine a woman feels frustrated because her partner doesn't provide emotional support when she's stressed at work. Instead of blaming her partner and trying to change him, she can apply Stoic principles and focus on what she can control: her own emotions and how she handles work stress. She can also practice mindfulness and reflection to better understand her own emotional needs and effectively communicate them to her partner.

Another example could be when a woman feels insecure in her relationship due to her partner's lack of communication and commitment. Instead of trying to control her partner to communicate more or change their behaviour, she can focus on what she can control: her own emotional reactions and how she expresses her needs to her partner. Practicing empathy and understanding towards her partner can also help strengthen the relationship and foster more open and honest communication.

In summary, applying Stoic principles in a romantic relationship can help women find the inner strength and tranquility to face challenges and find happiness in their love life. By practicing self-discipline, focusing on what they can control, and cultivating mindfulness and reflection, women can develop healthier and more meaningful relationships with their partners.

THE IMPORTANCE OF COMMUNICATION AND EMPATHY IN STOIC RELATIONSHIPS

Communication and empathy are two fundamental aspects of any romantic relationship, and Stoicism is no exception. Effective communication and empathetic understanding can help establish stronger and long-lasting relationships based on trust, respect, and mutual understanding.

In Stoicism, communication focuses on the clear and honest expression of feelings and thoughts, while avoiding anger and hostility. Empathy, on the other hand, involves the ability to put oneself in the other person's shoes, understand their feelings and concerns, and be compassionate towards their actions. Here are some examples of how to apply these principles in a romantic relationship:

1. Effective communication:

At times, it can be challenging to express our feelings clearly and effectively, especially when we are emotionally charged. In such cases, practicing assertive communication can be helpful, which means speaking directly, honestly, and respectfully, avoiding aggressive or passive tones. It is also important to actively listen to the other person, paying attention to their words and showing genuine interest in what they say.

2. Empathy:

Empathy is crucial for building a strong and fulfilling relationship. By putting oneself in the other person's shoes, it becomes easier to understand their needs and feelings, enabling greater understanding and collaboration in decision-making. For example, if your partner is going through a difficult time at work, it is important to demonstrate empathy and support by asking how they feel and offering assistance where necessary.

3. Avoiding hostility:

Stoicism also emphasizes the importance of avoiding anger and hostility in interpersonal relationships, as these emotions can be detrimental to communication and emotional connection. Instead, it is helpful to practice patience, understanding, and mutual respect, acknowledging that each person has their own perspective and needs.

In summary, communication and empathy are essential in a Stoic-based romantic relationship. By practicing effective communication, showing empathy, and avoiding hostility, it is possible to establish a strong and lasting relationship based on mutual understanding and respect.

HOW TO MAINTAIN A HEALTHY AND BALANCED RELATIONSHIP FROM A STOIC PERSPECTIVE

From a Stoic perspective, maintaining a healthy and balanced relationship involves applying philosophical principles of self-control, moderation, and reason. These principles can help women have more harmonious and satisfying relationships with their partners.

Firstly, self-control entails managing emotions and not allowing oneself to be carried away by them in moments of tension or conflict in the relationship. Women can practice self-discipline and patience in difficult situations, avoiding impulsive reactions that may worsen the situation. For example, instead of arguing with their partner when feeling angry, a Stoic woman can take a moment to breathe deeply and think before speaking.

Secondly, moderation is essential to maintain a balanced and healthy relationship. Stoic women can avoid falling into emotional extremes or overly demanding behaviors, which can jeopardize the stability of the relationship. For example, a Stoic woman may strive to find a balance in the relationship, avoiding being overly controlling or excessively passive.

Lastly, reason is fundamental in the relationship. Women can apply reason and logic to resolve conflicts in the relationship and maintain a clear and objective perspective. For example, if the couple is going through a difficult time, a Stoic woman may seek practical solutions and focus on the positive aspects of the relationship.

In summary, applying Stoic principles in a relationship can help women maintain a clear perspective, control emotions, and find a healthy balance in the relationship. The practice of self-control, moderation, and reason can be a powerful tool for building strong and satisfying relationships.

6. STOICISM, SEXUALITY, AND INTIMACY

"Do not let your thoughts become your actions; control your actions with your reason." - Marcus Aurelius

Stoicism is not only about attaining inner peace and emotional self-control but also understanding and properly managing our intimate relationships. In this chapter, we will focus on the Stoic perspective of sexuality and intimacy from a women's standpoint. We will explore how Stoic teachings can help women develop a healthier and more satisfying relationship with their own sexuality as well as with their partners. Additionally, we will discuss how Stoicism can assist in overcoming common obstacles in intimacy and cultivating a deep emotional connection with our partners.

STOICISM AND SEXUALITY: FINDING SELF-DISCIPLINE AND SELF-ACCEPTANCE

Stoicism is a philosophy that teaches us to find self-discipline and self-acceptance in various aspects of our lives, and sexuality is no exception. From a Stoic perspective, sexuality is seen as a natural and healthy aspect of human life, but one that requires self-control and self-acceptance to achieve a healthy balance.

For women, applying Stoic principles to sexuality can be particularly valuable, as they often face cultural and societal pressures that can affect their self-esteem and their relationship with their bodies and sexuality. Some practical examples of how Stoicism can help women find self-discipline and self-acceptance in sexuality include:

1. Embracing the body:

In the context of sexuality, Stoicism emphasizes the importance of accepting and valuing our bodies as they are. This involves recognizing and appreciating the diversity of body shapes and sizes, freeing ourselves from society's imposed beauty standards. By practicing body acceptance, women can cultivate a healthier and more positive relationship with their own bodies, promoting greater confidence and satisfaction in their sexual life. An example of this could be learning to admire and celebrate the unique features of our bodies, recognizing that true beauty lies in authenticity and self-acceptance.

2. Practicing self-control:

Stoicism also invites us to develop self-discipline in our lives, including our sexuality. This involves being aware of our sexual desires and emotions and learning to channel them consciously and healthily. Women can apply this principle by setting personal boundaries, making informed decisions about their sexual activity, and maintaining a balance between their emotional and physical needs. An example of this could be practicing sexual abstinence when it feels inappropriate or setting clear boundaries in a sexual relationship to ensure that their needs and desires are respected.

3. Cultivating emotional intimacy:

Emotional intimacy plays a crucial role in sexual life and intimate relationships. Stoicism encourages us to cultivate a deep and meaningful emotional connection with our partner, based on trust, open communication, and empathy. Women can apply this principle by expressing their sexual needs and desires clearly and respectfully, as well as being emotionally present during sexual encounters. An example of this could be establishing moments of emotional intimacy with the partner, such as sincere conversations and active listening, that foster greater connection and mutual understanding.

In summary, Stoicism offers valuable principles to help women find self-discipline and self-acceptance in the realm of sexuality. By embracing the body, practicing self-control, and cultivating emotional intimacy, women can experience greater satisfaction and fulfillment in their sexual life. It is important to remember that each woman has her own path and definition of a fulfilling sexual life, and Stoicism provides tools to navigate that path with authenticity and self-respect.

The Importance of Communication and Consent in Sexual Life from a Stoic Perspective

From a Stoic perspective, communication and consent are fundamental in any sexual relationship. Stoicism values the virtue of justice, which entails being fair and respectful in our interactions with others. In the realm of sexuality, this means listening to the needs and desires of our partner and communicating our own needs and boundaries clearly and respectfully.

It is particularly important for women to have an active and clear voice in their sexual experiences, as they often face societal pressures and expectations that can make them feel uncomfortable or insecure in intimate situations. By cultivating communication and consent in our sexual relationships, women can find more confidence and self-acceptance in their experiences.

Some examples of how to apply these Stoic principles in sexual life could include:

1. Discussing expectations:

In a sexual relationship, each person's expectations may vary greatly. For instance, a woman may desire a deeper emotional connection with her partner, while her partner may be more focused on physical pleasure. It is important for both parties to openly discuss their expectations and be willing to compromise to ensure that both parties are satisfied.

2. Seeking consent:

Consent is a crucial aspect of any sexual encounter. Women should feel comfortable and safe in establishing their boundaries and asking for what they want. This may include seeking permission before touching or exploring certain areas of the body or establishing a signaling system to communicate if something feels uncomfortable or painful.

3. Embracing vulnerability:

Sexual intimacy can be an emotionally intense and vulnerable experience. Women should be willing to embrace and express their feelings, even if they fear judgment or rejection. From a Stoic perspective, accepting vulnerability can help women cultivate self-acceptance and self-discipline in their sexual lives.

4. Communicating our boundaries:

If a woman is not comfortable with certain sexual activities, it is important to communicate this to her partner. This way, healthy boundaries can be established and the needs and desires of both parties can be respected.

5. Listening to our partner's needs:

Just as it is important to communicate our own boundaries and needs, it is also important to be willing to listen to and understand our partner's needs and desires. This can help create a more balanced and satisfying sexual relationship for both parties.

6. Reflecting on our own beliefs and cultural expectations:

Women often feel pressured by societal expectations surrounding sex and sexuality. By reflecting on our own beliefs and challenging these expectations, we can find greater self-determination and self-acceptance in our sexual experiences.

In summary, communication and consent are crucial in any sexual relationship from a Stoic perspective. For women, cultivating an active and clear voice in their sexual experiences can promote self-determination and self-acceptance in intimacy.

HOW TO CULTIVATE HAPPINESS AND SEXUAL FULFILLMENT FROM A STOIC PERSPECTIVE

Stoicism is not only about self-discipline and self-control but also about the pursuit of happiness and fulfillment in all aspects of life, including sexuality. From a Stoic perspective, cultivating happiness and sexual fulfillment involves finding a balance between our sexual needs and desires and our responsibilities and ethical values.

For women, this can be particularly important as they have often been taught to suppress their sexual needs and desires. By applying Stoic principles to our sexual lives, we can learn to accept ourselves and our bodies, communicate clearly and effectively with our partners, and find a healthy balance between our sexual life and other areas of our life.

Some examples of how to cultivate happiness and sexual fulfillment from a Stoic perspective include:

1. Accepting our bodies and sexual needs:

Instead of feeling ashamed or judgmental about our sexual needs and desires, we can learn to accept and value our bodies and sexual needs as part of our humanity. This may involve working on self-acceptance and self-esteem and learning to communicate effectively with our partners.

2. Effective and respectful communication:

Effective communication and mutual respect are essential in any healthy sexual relationship. From a Stoic perspective, this involves being clear and direct in our communications, being respectful of our partner's needs and desires, and being open to listening and responding to their needs and desires as well.

3. Finding a healthy balance:

Stoicism teaches us to find balance in all areas of our life, and sexuality is no exception. Instead of solely focusing on our sexual life, we can find a healthy balance between our sexual life and other important areas of our life, such as family, friends, career, and our own emotional and physical needs.

In conclusion, cultivating happiness and sexual fulfilment from a Stoic perspective involves accepting ourselves and our sexual needs, communicating effectively and respectfully with our partners, and finding a healthy balance between our sexual life and other important areas of our life.

7. STOICISM AND MOTHERHOOD: CULTIVATING STRENGTH AND SERENITY

"Motherhood is the perfect opportunity to showcase the true greatness of the Stoic mind in action." - Epictetus

Motherhood is a journey filled with joys, challenges, and sacrifices. In this chapter, we will explore how Stoicism can be a valuable guide for women on their path as mothers. From learning to accept the realities of parenting to facing emotional challenges and finding serenity amidst chaos, Stoicism offers practical principles and enriching perspectives.

MOTHERHOOD AND STOICISM: FOUNDATIONS AND APPROACHES

Motherhood is a journey full of emotions, challenges, and joys. As women become mothers, they encounter situations that test their patience, resilience, and adaptability. Stoicism, an ancient philosophy of life, can provide valuable guidance for facing these challenges and cultivating the strength and serenity needed in raising children. In this section, we will explore the foundations and approaches of Stoicism in relation to motherhood, providing practical tools for women who wish to embrace their role as mothers with Stoic wisdom.

1. The role of acceptance in parenting:

Acceptance is a cornerstone of Stoicism and plays a crucial role in motherhood. It involves recognizing and embracing present circumstances, both the positive and challenging ones, and learning to find inner peace despite them. For example, a mother can practice acceptance when facing unforeseen situations, such as changes in routine or illnesses in her children. Instead of resisting and generating stress, she can apply Stoic principles of acceptance and adaptation to find creative solutions and maintain calm amidst chaos.

2. The virtue of moderation and balance in motherhood:

Stoicism promotes the virtue of moderation and balance in all areas of life, including motherhood. Being a Stoic mother involves finding the middle ground between extremes, such as overprotection and neglect, perfectionism and lack of self-care. For example, a Stoic mother can seek a healthy balance by setting clear boundaries with her children, giving them autonomy and fostering their growth while also taking care of herself and fulfilling her own needs.

3. How mindfulness can strengthen the mother-child

connection:

Mindfulness, a fundamental practice in Stoicism, can strengthen the connection between a mother and her child. Mindfulness involves being present in the current moment, without judgments or distractions. A Stoic mother can apply mindfulness by dedicating quality time with her child, appreciating each interaction, and creating a deep bond. For example, while playing with her child, she can focus all her attention on the play, without worrying about pending tasks or intrusive thoughts.

4. Cultivating resilience in the face of daily motherhood challenges:

Resilience is an invaluable skill in motherhood, and Stoicism provides tools to develop it. Being a Stoic mother involves recognising that challenges are a natural part of life and finding the inner strength to overcome them. For example, a Stoic mother can apply Stoic philosophy when facing the everyday difficulties of motherhood, such as lack of sleep, constant demands, and moments of exhaustion. Instead of being carried away by stress and frustration, she can practice self-discipline and remember that she has the power to choose her response to each situation. This will allow her to stay calm, find creative solutions, and move forward with determination.

In summary, Stoicism provides a solid framework for approaching motherhood with wisdom and serenity. Through acceptance, moderation, mindfulness, and resilience, mothers can find balance, cultivate a deeper connection with their children, and develop a resilient mindset to overcome daily challenges.

Stoicism does not seek to deny emotions or minimise the importance of motherhood but rather provides practical tools for facing the ups and downs of this life experience. By embracing Stoic principles, women can find a sense of empowerment and self-reflection that allows them to fully embrace their role as mothers and find fulfilment in their journey.

Ultimately, Stoicism invites mothers to seek virtue and happiness in their role of nurturing and raising their children while reminding them that they are also valuable individuals with their own needs and desires. By balancing these dualities and finding their own inner strength, mothers can build a solid foundation for their own well-being and that of their families.

As the Stoic Seneca once said, "It is not because things are difficult that we do not dare, it is because we do not dare that they are difficult." So, dear mothers, have the courage to embrace Stoic philosophy in your motherhood journey, and you will discover a strength and serenity that will allow you to flourish with gratitude and fulfilment.

May Stoic wisdom illuminate and guide the path of all mothers, strengthening their resilience and enabling them to find fulfillment in the wonderful experience of being mothers!

MOTHERHOOD AND PERSONAL CHOICE

Motherhood is a central theme in the lives of many women. However, in the modern era, it is increasingly recognized that motherhood is not a universal experience or an obligation for all women. There are diverse perspectives, choices, and experiences surrounding motherhood, and it is important to approach them from a Stoic perspective.

In this section, we will explore how Stoicism can provide a framework of understanding and support for women in relation to motherhood and personal choice. Recognizing that every woman has the right to decide whether or not she wants to be a mother, we will address three fundamental aspects: women who do not desire to be mothers, facing societal judgments and expectations about motherhood, and seeking one's own identity and purpose beyond motherhood.

Through these sections, we will reflect on the challenges and opportunities that arise when making decisions related to motherhood, and how Stoicism can offer support and guidance in finding authenticity and fulfillment in each woman's life. We will acknowledge that personal value and fulfillment are not limited to motherhood but extend to multiple aspects of a woman's life.

Let us embark on this fascinating journey of exploration and discovery, and uncover how Stoicism can be a compass to navigate the complexities of motherhood and personal choice, opening new horizons of empowerment and growth.

1. Women who do not desire to be mothers: Respecting and accepting individual choice

Every woman has the right to make decisions about her own life and the path she wishes to pursue. Some women may choose not to be mothers, and this choice should be respected and accepted without judgment or external pressure. Stoicism teaches us to value autonomy and self-determination, recognizing that each individual has their own desires, goals, and purpose in life.

It is important for women who do not desire to be mothers to find support and understanding from their surroundings. When facing questions or criticism about their choice, they can practice self-discipline and moderation in their responses, avoiding getting into unproductive arguments. Instead of trying to convince others or defend their position, they can focus on living their lives according to their own values and goals.

Example: Maria has decided that she does not want to have children and faces constant pressure from her family and friends, who question her choice and tell her that she will change her mind in the future. Maria practices self-discipline by not letting frustration and anger consume her. Instead, she focuses on her own personal growth and living a fulfilling life according to her own goals and passions. Through Stoicism, she finds the strength to stand firm in her choice and surrounds herself with people who support and respect her decision.

2. Facing societal judgments and expectations about motherhood

Motherhood carries a set of expectations and societal judgments rooted in culture and established norms. Women who choose to be mothers may face pressures to conform to certain standards or predefined roles. However, Stoicism teaches us not to allow external opinions to define our worth or identity.

It is crucial for women to recognize that their worth and sense of purpose do not depend solely on their role as mothers. They can practice self-acceptance and cultivate their own identity beyond motherhood. This involves acknowledging and honoring their passions, talents, and individual goals, and finding a healthy balance between being a mother and pursuing their own dreams.

Example: Laura is a mother and also a talented artist. However, she feels pressured by society and the expectations of being a "perfect mother" and sacrificing her artistic career. Through Stoicism, Laura develops the ability to accept her worth as both a mother and an artist equally. She frees herself from external judgments and finds motivation to dedicate time to her artistic passion, knowing that this also contributes to her personal growth and overall happiness.

3. Finding one's own identity and purpose beyond motherhood

While motherhood can be a transformative and fulfilling experience, it is also important for women to find and cultivate their own identities and purposes beyond their role as mothers. Stoicism invites us to recognise that we are individual beings with multiple dimensions and potentials, and that our personal fulfilment is not solely limited to motherhood.

To find their own identity and purpose, women can explore different areas of interest, pursue their passions, and set personal goals. They can seek opportunities for growth and development both professionally and personally. Additionally, they can harness the power of self-discipline and focus on what they can control to overcome challenges and obstacles that may arise along their path.

Example: Andrea is a mother of two children and also has a strong interest in volunteering and community service. Through Stoicism, she recognises the importance of cultivating her identity beyond her role as a mother. Andrea dedicates time to participate in nonprofit organisations and finds fulfilment in helping others. By focusing on her purpose and living according to her values, Andrea achieves a balance between her role as a mother and her individual passions.

In conclusion, Stoicism invites us to embrace the diversity of choices and decisions in motherhood. It recognizes the value of self-determination and respect for individual choices. Women can find strength and motivation in Stoicism to embrace their choice of not being mothers, face societal judgments related to motherhood, and find their own identity and purpose beyond their role as mothers. Ultimately, Stoicism inspires us to live an authentic, fulfilling, and meaningful life where each woman can find her own path to happiness and personal fulfillment.

"Blossom in your own essence, find your purpose, and embrace the fullness of your life beyond imposed roles and expectations. You are a strong, valuable woman capable of creating your own happiness."

MOTHERHOOD AND INFERTILITY: CULTIVATING RESILIENCE AND HOPE

Motherhood is a path filled with expectations, dreams, and longings for many women. However, in some cases, this path can be marked by the challenge of infertility. The inability to conceive naturally can bring about pain, frustration, and a profound sense of loss. In these difficult moments, Stoicism can be a guiding light that leads us towards resilience and hope.

In this section, we will explore the intersection between motherhood and infertility from a Stoic perspective. We will address three fundamental aspects: how to cope with the pain and frustration of infertility, the power of acceptance and adaptation in assisted fertility processes, and how to find fulfillment and personal fulfillment beyond biological motherhood.

The path of infertility can be arduous and filled with emotional and physical obstacles. However, by adopting Stoic principles, we can find the inner strength needed to navigate this situation. We will learn to embrace reality as it is, practice acceptance, and adapt to changing circumstances. Instead of solely focusing on biological motherhood, we will open ourselves to new ways of finding fulfilment and purpose in our lives.

Motherhood is not solely defined by the ability to conceive and give birth to a child. Motherhood is a state of love, care, and connection, and it can manifest in various forms, including adoption, fostering, or dedicating oneself to other forms of care and support. By cultivating resilience and hope, we can find fulfilment and personal growth beyond biological limitations.

Let us embark on this journey of exploration and discover how Stoicism can help us find strength, acceptance, and hope amidst infertility. Let us open our minds and hearts to new possibilities and realise that motherhood is a path of love and fulfilment, regardless of the circumstances surrounding us.

1. Coping with the pain and frustration of infertility

Facing infertility can be an emotionally devastating experience. Women who desire to be mothers but cannot conceive naturally often experience feelings of sadness, loss, and despair. In this journey, Stoicism can provide tools to confront pain and frustration with resilience and hope.

An example of facing the pain and frustration of infertility from a Stoic perspective is practicing acceptance of reality. Instead of clinging to unrealistic expectations or focusing on what cannot be controlled, a woman can cultivate acceptance of her situation and learn to find meaning and beauty in other areas of her life. This involves recognizing that infertility does not define her worth as a woman and mother, and that there are many ways to experience motherhood and love.

2. The power of acceptance and adaptation in the process of assisted fertility

When infertility leads to seeking assisted fertility options such as in vitro fertilisation or artificial insemination, Stoicism can help women confront this process with acceptance and adaptation. Assisted fertility entails facing physical, emotional, and financial challenges and can bring about a rollercoaster of hopes and disappointments.

An example of applying Stoicism in the process of assisted fertility is cultivating a resilient and flexible mindset. Women can learn to adapt to the emotional ups and downs and the obstacles that may arise along the way. They can focus on what they can control, such as following medical recommendations, taking care of themselves, and maintaining a positive attitude towards the circumstances. Through acceptance and adaptation, they strengthen themselves and maintain hope even in the most challenging times.

3. Finding fulfilment and personal growth beyond biological motherhood

For those women who cannot conceive or choose not to have children, Stoicism can also serve as a powerful guide to finding fulfilment and personal growth in other aspects of their lives. Biological motherhood is not the sole source of love, purpose, and satisfaction in a woman's life.

An example of finding personal fulfillment and fulfillment beyond biological motherhood is to focus on projects and goals that bring joy and meaning. A woman can discover passions, develop her professional career, establish deep relationships, and contribute to the well-being of her community. By recognizing that motherhood does not define her worth and that there are multiple ways to find purpose and satisfaction, she can liberate herself from societal stereotypes and expectations and create a meaningful and gratifying life.

Let us remember that motherhood is a personal choice, and every woman has the right to decide her own path. Stoicism invites us to embrace reality as it is.

THE IMPORTANCE OF SELF-CARE IN MOTHERHOOD

Motherhood is a journey filled with love, dedication, and responsibilities. However, mothers often forget to take care of themselves amidst the demands and needs of their children. Self-care in motherhood is essential for the physical and emotional well-being of the mother, and Stoicism can provide valuable approaches to prioritize personal care in this stage of life.

1. Prioritizing the Physical and Emotional Well-being of the Mother

- Focusing on the physical and emotional well-being of the mother is crucial for her ability to care for her family. Stoicism reminds us that by taking care of ourselves, we are better equipped to care for others. Some Stoic practices for physical and emotional self-care could include:

- Establishing routines of exercise and healthy eating, even when time and energy are limited. For example, dedicating a few minutes each day to stretching, practicing yoga, or taking a walk in nature.
Cultivating gratitude and mindfulness, finding moments to appreciate the small things and reconnect with oneself. For example, keeping a gratitude journal or practicing meditation for a few minutes each day.

2. The Need to Set Boundaries and Seek Help

Motherhood can be overwhelming, and it is important to recognize that one cannot do everything alone. Setting boundaries and seeking help when needed is an act of self-care and a display of strength. Some practical examples could be:

- Delegating tasks and responsibilities in household and childcare, involving partners, family members, or close friends. For example, asking for help with household chores, child care, or meal preparation.

- Establishing clear boundaries regarding time and energy, reserving moments to rest, relax, and engage in activities that bring joy and personal rejuvenation. For example, scheduling time to read a book, practice a hobby, or enjoy a relaxing bath.

3. The Connection between Self-Reflection and Conscious Parenting

Self-reflection is a powerful tool for conscious parenting. Stoicism invites us to examine our actions and emotions, and to cultivate wisdom and self-transcendence. Some practical examples could be:

- Taking moments of self-reflection to evaluate our reactions and responses in parenting our children, seeking areas of improvement and personal growth. For example, asking oneself how to be a more patient, understanding, and present mother.
- Practicing emotional self-control and stress management, recognizing that our emotions have an impact on our children. For example, seeking relaxation techniques such as deep breathing or visualization to maintain calmness in challenging situations.

Self-care in motherhood not only benefits the mother but also has a positive impact on the children and the overall family dynamics. A mother who takes care of herself is capable of providing love, attention, and support more effectively. By prioritizing her physical and emotional well-being, setting boundaries and seeking help when needed, and practicing self-reflection, the mother becomes a role model of self-care and conscious parenting for her children.

It is important to remember that self-care is not selfishness but an investment in our own well-being and that of our family. By practicing Stoicism in motherhood, we can find a balance between the demands of parenting and our own needs, creating a harmonious and healthy environment for everyone involved.

In summary, self-care in motherhood is essential for the health and well-being of the mother, as well as the emotional development of the children. By prioritizing physical and emotional well-being, setting boundaries and seeking help, and practicing self-reflection, the mother can cultivate conscious and balanced motherhood. Remember that taking care of yourself is an act of love towards yourself and your family, and it allows you to flourish in all aspects of your life. Embracing self-care and drawing wisdom from Stoicism can empower mothers to navigate the challenges of motherhood with resilience, fulfillment, and a sense of purpose.

STOICISM AND THE DEVELOPMENT OF VALUES IN CHILDREN

Raising children is one of life's most important and rewarding responsibilities. As parents, we seek to guide our children towards healthy growth and development, as well as instill in them strong values that will help them navigate life's challenges. In this section, we will explore how Stoicism can be a valuable tool in promoting the development of values in our children.

1. Teaching children Stoic principles such as self-discipline and self-control:

Teaching our children Stoic principles such as self-discipline and self-control equips them with the necessary tools to face temptations, overcome obstacles, and make responsible decisions. We can foster self-discipline by setting clear boundaries, establishing realistic goals, and helping them develop a routine that promotes balance and responsibility. For example, encouraging our children to establish regular study schedules and resist distractions will teach them the importance of self-discipline in the pursuit of academic success.

2. Promoting resilience and acceptance of adversity:

Life is full of challenges and setbacks, and it is important for our children to learn how to face them with resilience and acceptance. We can foster resilience by encouraging them to view failures as learning opportunities and by urging them to persevere despite difficulties. For instance, if our child experiences a sports disappointment, we can help them reflect on what happened, find valuable lessons in the experience, and encourage them to move forward with determination.

3. Encouraging gratitude and focusing on what can be controlled:

Stoicism teaches us to value what we have and focus on what is within our control. We can promote gratitude in our children by teaching them to appreciate the simple things in life and encouraging them to express gratitude for their blessings. Additionally, we can help them recognize that they cannot control all circumstances, but they can control their attitude and response to them. For example, encouraging our children to find creative solutions to problems and adapt to changes will help them develop a resilient mindset focused on what they can control.

In conclusion, Stoicism can serve as a valuable guide in raising our children, helping them develop strong values and face life's challenges with resilience, self-discipline, and gratitude. By teaching them these principles and providing practical examples, we are preparing them to become strong and mindful adults. Let us remember that our children are sponges that absorb our attitudes and behaviors, so being a Stoic role model and imparting these values will have a positive influence on their growth and development.

> *"Raising our children with Stoic principles is sowing in them the seeds of inner strength and the necessary wisdom to face life's challenges with courage and serenity. By guiding them towards self-discipline, resilience, and focusing on what they can control, we are providing them with powerful tools to build a future filled with success, happiness, and fulfillment. May our teachings and examples inspire our children to become strong, compassionate individuals capable of finding greatness within themselves.".*

Remember, as parents, we have the privilege and responsibility to shape the character and future of our children. Through Stoicism, we can provide them with the foundation for a meaningful and resilient life. Let us keep the flame of Stoicism alive in our upbringing and inspire future generations to live with authenticity and wisdom.

This section of the book has led us to explore the importance of transmitting Stoic principles to our children and fostering their personal and moral development. Throughout this topic, we have addressed different fundamental aspects to cultivate solid values and a resilient mindset in them.

Firstly, we have emphasized the importance of teaching our children Stoic principles such as self-discipline and self-control. We provide them with the opportunity to learn how to manage their emotions and actions, make decisions based on reason, and resist temptations that may undermine their long-term well-being. For example, we teach them to establish study schedules, control their impulses, and delay gratification to achieve more meaningful goals.

Secondly, we have highlighted the need to foster resilience and acceptance of adversity in our children. We teach them to face challenges with courage and determination, view obstacles as opportunities for growth, and find valuable lessons even in the most difficult moments. For instance, we show them how to learn from failures, how to adapt to unexpected changes, and how to find creative solutions to problems.

Thirdly, we have emphasized the importance of promoting gratitude and focusing on what can be controlled in our children's lives. We teach them to appreciate what they have, value the simple things in life, and cultivate an abundance mindset. Additionally, we teach them to recognize that there are situations beyond their control but they can control their attitude and response to them. For example, encouraging our children to find creative solutions to problems and adapt to changes will help them develop a resilient mindset focused on what they can control.

By developing these values and skills in our children, we provide them with a solid foundation to face life's challenges with wisdom and strength. We are preparing them to be individuals of integrity, capable of making informed decisions, facing adversity with resilience, and finding happiness in their own capacity for self-transcendence.

In conclusion, Stoicism can offer valuable guidance in raising our children, helping them develop solid values and face life's challenges with resilience, self-discipline, and gratitude. By teaching them these principles and providing practical examples, we are preparing them to be strong and mindful adults. Let us remember that our children are sponges that absorb our attitudes and behaviors, so being a Stoic role model and transmitting these values will be a positive influence on their growth and development.

In this comprehensive analysis of "Motherhood and Stoicism," we have explored various foundations and approaches that can enrich the experience of being a mother. Through the different points discussed, we have discovered valuable lessons that allow us to cultivate motherhood based on acceptance, personal choice, resilience, and the development of solid values in our children.

Firstly, we have reflected on the fundamental role of acceptance in parenting. Recognizing and embracing the reality of motherhood, with its joys and challenges, provides us with an opportunity to find serenity and develop a positive mindset in any circumstance. Acceptance allows us to flow with the experience, adapt to changes, and respond in a wiser and more conscious manner.

Additionally, we have explored the virtue of moderation and balance in motherhood. The ability to set boundaries and maintain a balanced life helps us avoid exhaustion and cultivate a harmonious environment for ourselves and our children. Moderation enables us to discern our priorities, consciously distribute our energies, and live an authentic and healthy motherhood.

Mindfulness has emerged as a powerful tool for strengthening the mother-child connection. By practicing mindfulness, we can be present and aware in every moment shared with our children, nurturing a deep and meaningful connection. Mindfulness invites us to savor each moment, listen with empathy, and respond with compassion, creating an atmosphere of love and mutual understanding.

Resilience has proven to be an invaluable resource in the everyday challenges of motherhood. Facing pain, frustration, and uncertainty with resilience allows us to find inner strength and overcome obstacles with determination. Resilience helps us model an attitude of perseverance and adaptability in the face of difficulties, providing a solid foundation to guide and support our children in their own development.

Furthermore, we have explored the importance of self-care in motherhood. Prioritizing our physical and emotional well-being allows us to be in optimal conditions to care for and nurture our children. Setting healthy boundaries, seeking help when necessary, and cultivating self-reflection help us maintain a balanced state and develop mindful and loving parenting.

Finally, we have explored how Stoicism can contribute to the development of values in our children. Teaching them Stoic principles such as self-discipline, resilience, acceptance of adversity, gratitude, and focusing on what can be controlled provides them with a solid foundation to face life's challenges with wisdom and strength. By imparting these teachings, we equip them with tools to build a meaningful and fulfilling life.

In conclusion, "Motherhood and Stoicism" invites us to reflect on the wonderful and complex journey of being a mother and offers us tools and perspectives from Stoicism to approach this role in a more conscious and enriching way. Through acceptance, personal choice, resilience, self-care, and the development of values in our children, we can transform our experience as mothers and raise our children in a more balanced, loving, and wise manner.

It is important to remember that every woman experiences motherhood uniquely, and there is no single "correct" way to be a mother. Recognizing and respecting the individual choice of women who do not wish to be mothers invites us to build a more inclusive society free from judgment. Similarly, facing societal judgments and expectations about motherhood challenges us to find our own identity and purpose beyond this role, opening paths to personal fulfillment and empowerment.

The experience of infertility can be painful and challenging, requiring a great deal of resilience. Facing frustration and pain, accepting and adapting to circumstances, and finding fulfillment and personal realization beyond biological motherhood are fundamental aspects of navigating this path with strength and hope.

Self-care emerges as an essential need in motherhood, as we can only care for and nurture our children when we care for ourselves. Prioritizing our physical and emotional well-being, setting healthy boundaries, and seeking support allow us to be more balanced and present mothers, creating a positive impact on our children.

Moreover, fostering open communication with our children is crucial in motherhood. Encouraging dialogue, active listening, and empathy creates a safe and trusting space for them to express themselves and develop their own unique voices. By nurturing open communication, we foster healthy relationships and empower our children to become confident and self-aware individuals.

In the end, "Motherhood and Stoicism" is an invitation to embark on a transformative journey of self-discovery and conscious parenting. By incorporating Stoic principles into our lives, such as acceptance, resilience, self-care, and the development of values, we can navigate the challenges of motherhood with wisdom and grace. Let us embrace our role as mothers with love, authenticity, and a commitment to nurturing the well-being and growth of our children. May our journey as mothers be a source of inspiration and empowerment for ourselves and future generations.

8. STOICISM AND LESBIAN WOMAN

*"Happiness does not depend on external things, but on
the way we interpret them." - Epictetus*

In today's world, sexual diversity is becoming increasingly accepted, but there is still much work to be done to eradicate stigma and discrimination. Stoicism can be a valuable tool for lesbian women seeking to accept their identity and live fully regardless of others' opinions. In this chapter, we will explore how Stoic principles can help lesbian women find happiness and authenticity in their lives and relationships.

APPLYING STOIC PRINCIPLES TO THE LIFE OF A LESBIAN WOMAN

1. The Principle of Wisdom and Reason:

This principle is about seeking truth and knowledge to make informed decisions. In the context of a lesbian woman, this means having a clear and honest understanding of her sexual orientation and what it means to her. Instead of hiding her sexuality or feeling ashamed of it, the lesbian woman can embrace and accept it as part of her identity.

Practical example: A lesbian woman can seek information and resources about the LGBT+ community to learn more about her identity and connect with other community members.

2. The Principle of Fortitude and Resilience:

This principle is about having the mental and emotional strength to face challenges and overcome them. In the context of a lesbian woman, this means having the ability to deal with discrimination, homophobia, and rejection while staying true to her identity and beliefs.

Practical example: A lesbian woman can find support in understanding friends and family, participate in LGBT+ groups and organizations to feel part of a broader community, and practice meditation and mindfulness techniques to strengthen her mind and spirit.

3. The Principle of Justice and Equity:

This principle is about being fair and equitable in our actions and relationships. In the context of a lesbian woman, this means treating everyone with equality and respect, regardless of their sexual orientation.

Practical example: A lesbian woman can educate friends and family who may have unconscious biases about the LGBT + community and speak out against discrimination and homophobia in her daily life.

4. The Principle of Moderation and Temperance:

This principle is about finding a balance between our desires and needs. In the context of a lesbian woman, this means finding a balance between her sexual identity and the demands and expectations of society.

Practical example: A lesbian woman can practice self-reflection and self-understanding to find a balance between her own needs and desires and societal expectations. She can make informed decisions about her love and sexual life without feeling obligated to conform to social or familial norms.

5. The Principle of Gratitude and Acceptance:

This principle is about appreciating what we have and accepting what we cannot change. In the context of a lesbian woman, this means appreciating and accepting her sexual identity and the loving and sexual relationships that are a part of it.

Practical example: A lesbian woman can practice gratitude and acceptance by focusing on the loving and sexual relationships she has built and the positive experiences she has had. She can work on accepting any discrimination or rejection she may have faced.

By applying these Stoic principles, lesbian women can navigate the challenges they may encounter, embrace their true selves, and find happiness and fulfillment in their lives and relationships. Stoicism provides a guiding philosophy that empowers individuals to live authentically and unapologetically, irrespective of societal expectations or prejudices.

THE IMPORTANCE OF SELF-ACCEPTANCE AND RESILIENCE IN LESBIAN STOICISM

Lesbian Stoicism is about accepting oneself, including all aspects of one's identity, including sexual orientation. Self-acceptance is crucial for cultivating resilience and emotional strength that are necessary to face the challenges and difficulties that arise in life.

One of the key Stoic principles in self-acceptance is the acceptance of reality. This entails accepting things that cannot be changed and working to change those that can. In the context of sexual orientation, this means accepting that one is a lesbian and working towards living an authentic and fulfilling life.

Another important Stoic principle is emotional fortitude. This involves developing the ability to stand firm in the face of adversity and intense emotions. In the context of sexual orientation, this means confronting prejudice and discrimination with strength and resilience.

A third Stoic principle relevant to self-acceptance and resilience is empathy. This entails developing the ability to put oneself in the shoes of others and understand their perspective. In the context of sexual orientation, this means having empathy for the experiences of other LGBTQ+ community members and supporting those who are struggling with accepting their identity.

Lastly, the Stoic principle of character ethics is relevant to self-acceptance and resilience. This involves developing ethical virtues such as honesty, integrity, and compassion. In the context of sexual orientation, this means living in accordance with personal and ethical values and being true to oneself.

Some practical examples of applying these principles in the life of a lesbian woman could include:

- Practicing acceptance of reality by recognizing that sexual orientation is a fundamental part of one's identity and working to create an authentic and meaningful life accordingly.
- Developing emotional fortitude by facing prejudice and discrimination through seeking support from understanding friends and family, building an LGBTQ+ community, and engaging in self-care.
- Practicing empathy with other LGBTQ+ community members and supporting them in their own journey of acceptance and resilience.
- Cultivating ethical virtues such as honesty, integrity, and compassion by living in accordance with personal and ethical values and being true to oneself.

FINDING HAPPINESS AND PERSONAL FULFILLMENT IN A SOCIETY OFTEN HOSTILE TO THE LGBT COMMUNITY

Finding happiness and personal fulfillment in a society that is not always welcoming to the LGBT community can be challenging, but Stoicism can help us face it with courage and perseverance.

It is important to note that every culture and society has its own attitudes and prejudices towards the LGBT community, and some places may be more accepting than others. For example, in some countries, same-sex marriage is legal, while in others, it is illegal and may even be punishable by law. Attitudes towards the LGBT community can also vary among different religious groups, age groups, and generations

However, regardless of the society we live in, we can apply Stoic principles to find happiness and personal fulfillment in our lives. We can develop our capacity for self-acceptance and resilience by embracing our authenticity and living according to our values.

To find happiness and personal fulfillment, we can focus on what we can control and accept what we cannot. We can work on our self-acceptance and build a strong and authentic identity. We can also cultivate resilience by developing our ability to face adversity and overcome obstacles.

For example, a lesbian woman living in a conservative society that does not accept sexual diversity can apply Stoic principles to find happiness and personal fulfillment. She can work on her self-acceptance by embracing her sexuality and building a strong and authentic identity. She can also cultivate resilience by developing her ability to face adversity and overcome obstacles. She can seek support from friendly and supportive LGBT communities and find creative ways to live her life according to her values and desires, even if it means facing discrimination and exclusion.

9. CONCLUSION

"The greatest achievement of a woman is not in how her
life is shaped, but in how she faces adversity and finds
inner peace in the midst of the storm." - Seneca

As we reach the end of this journey through stoicism and its relevance for women in the modern era, it is evident that we have explored a path of strength, resilience, and self-determination. We have discovered how stoic principles can transform our lives, allowing us to embrace our authenticity, find inner peace, and build healthy and balanced relationships.

Throughout these pages, we have learned to live according to reason, to practice self-discipline, and to cultivate resilience in the face of everyday challenges. We have understood the importance of focusing on what we can control and living fully in the present moment, freeing ourselves from worries and anxieties that prevent us from enjoying life.

We have explored the practical application of stoicism in different areas of our lives, from work and school to family life and romantic relationships. We have learned to communicate with empathy, establish healthy boundaries, and cultivate happiness and sexual fulfillment from a stoic perspective.

Furthermore, we have addressed the importance of self-determination, independence, and self-acceptance in women's lives. We have challenged stereotypes and cultural limitations, reaffirming our femininity without compromising our authenticity.

In this journey, we have given special attention to lesbian women, recognizing their unique experience and the importance of self-acceptance and resilience in their path to happiness and personal fulfillment. We have addressed the challenges they face in an often hostile society and offered them tools and perspectives to find inner strength and live authentically.

So, dear women, let stoicism be your guide in this journey of empowerment and self-discovery. Remember that you have the ability to face any obstacle and find the inner strength to overcome it. Be true to yourselves, cultivate resilience, and embrace your personal power.

In the words of a stoic sage, *"The power is within you; control your thoughts and you will be invincible."* Trust in your ability to face challenges with wisdom and serenity, and embrace every moment of your life with gratitude and purpose.

Always remember that you are the authors of your own story, capable of building a fulfilling and satisfying life. May your path be filled with joy, love, and fulfillment!

> *"The power is within you; control your thoughts and you will be invincible." - Marcus Aurelius.*

SUMMARY OF STOIC PRINCIPLES AND THEIR RELEVANCE FOR WOMEN IN THE MODERN ERA

In this final section of the book, a summary of the stoic principles that have been addressed throughout the work is provided, reflecting on their relevance for women in the modern era.

First and foremost, the importance of self-discipline and self-control is highlighted as fundamental tools for achieving a fulfilling and satisfying life. Women, in particular, have historically faced many restrictions and limitations in terms of autonomy and decision-making. However, stoicism reminds us that regardless of external circumstances, we always have the ability to control our own thoughts and actions.

Secondly, the significance of self-acceptance and self-compassion is emphasized. Modern society often imposes ideals of beauty, behavior, and gender roles that can be restrictive and limiting for women. Stoicism teaches us to value our own qualities and strengths, and to accept our limitations and weaknesses without harsh self-judgment.

Thirdly, the importance of effective communication and constructive dialogue in our interpersonal relationships is emphasized. Women, like any other social group, often face barriers in communication and expressing their thoughts and feelings. Stoicism urges us to be clear and honest in our communications, and to always seek mutual understanding and respect in our relationships.

Fourthly, the significance of resilience and the ability to face life's challenges with determination and strength is highlighted. Women have historically faced many forms of discrimination and violence, and often encounter additional barriers in their pursuit of happiness and personal fulfillment. Stoicism reminds us that, despite the challenges and difficulties, we can always find the strength and resilience to confront and overcome them.

In summary, stoicism offers valuable tools for women to cultivate a fulfilling and satisfying life in the modern era. Through self-discipline, self-acceptance, effective communication, and resilience, we can confront the challenges of life with determination and strength, and find the happiness and personal fulfillment we seek.

PRACTICAL STEPS TO APPLY STOIC PRINCIPLES IN DAILY LIFE

Stoic principles are a valuable guide to living a fulfilling and satisfying life in any era, and they are equally applicable to women in the modern era. However, theory alone is not enough to transform our lives; we must turn principles into concrete actions to experience their true power. Here are some practical steps to apply stoic principles in daily life:

1. Practice self-discipline: Self-discipline is the foundation of stoicism. To start, begin with small goals such as waking up early or exercising daily, and gradually increase the difficulty. By doing this, you will strengthen your ability to resist temptation and stay true to your principles.

2. Practice mindfulness: Mindfulness is the practice of living in the present moment and paying attention to your thoughts and feelings. Meditation is a valuable tool for developing mindfulness. Start with short meditations and gradually increase the time you spend meditating.

3. Cultivate resilience: Life is full of challenges and adversities. Resilience is the ability to bounce back from difficulties. One way to develop resilience is to view obstacles as opportunities for growth and learning rather than being defeated by them.

4. Practice gratitude: Gratitude is a powerful emotion that helps us focus on what we have rather than what is lacking. Take a moment every day to reflect on what you are grateful for in your life.

5. Practice emotional detachment: Stoicism teaches us not to become emotionally attached to external things like wealth or prestige. Instead, we should focus on what we can control: our actions and thoughts. Learn to accept what is beyond your control and focus on what you can change.

6. Practice compassion: Compassion is the practice of caring for the well-being of others. Treat others with kindness and respect, even when they may not deserve it. Additionally, learn to forgive and free yourself from the burden of resentment.

7. Practice practical wisdom: Practical wisdom is the ability to apply stoic principles in practical situations of everyday life. This requires the constant practice of reflecting on our actions and thoughts and determining if they align with our values and principles.

In summary, stoic principles offer a valuable guide to living a fulfilling and satisfying life in the modern era. By practicing self-discipline, mindfulness, resilience, gratitude, emotional detachment, compassion, and practical wisdom, we can turn principles into concrete actions and experience their true power.

INSPIRATION FOR LIVING A FULFILLING AND SATISFYING LIFE THROUGH STOICISM

Stoicism invites us to live a fulfilling and satisfying life by accepting the world as it is and developing our virtue to face life's challenges. As women, we can find inspiration in Stoic teachings to achieve our happiness and well-being.

One key to a Stoic life is the cultivation of self-discipline and self-acceptance. We must accept our strengths and weaknesses and work on constant self-improvement. We must also learn to differentiate what is within our control and what is not, to avoid worrying about what we cannot change and focus on what we can do.

Another important principle is the significance of connection and community. Women can find support and solidarity in other community members while offering their own help and support. Through connection and fellowship, we can find strength and inspiration to face life's challenges.

Lastly, we must remember that life is a constant process of learning and growth. Stoicism encourages us to view life's challenges as opportunities to grow and improve as individuals. As women, we can find inspiration in this perspective to seek our own personal fulfillment and achieve our goals and objectives.

In summary, Stoicism offers us a practical philosophy for living a fulfilling and satisfying life. Women can find inspiration in Stoic principles to cultivate self-discipline, self-acceptance, and connection with the community. Life is a constant journey of learning and growth, and Stoicism invites us to embrace this truth and find happiness and personal fulfillment.

"Remember, you can control your life and find your path to happiness and fulfillment! You are the master of your destiny!"

ACKNOWLEDGMENTS

Celebrating Life, Support, and Inspiration

In this moment of gratitude and reflection, I want to express my deep appreciation to all the individuals and influences that have contributed to the creation of this book. Through these words, I want to honor and acknowledge life itself, as well as those who have shared their wisdom, support, and love on my journey.

I am grateful to life for every experience, every challenge, and every triumph. Each step has been an opportunity for growth, learning, and evolution. I appreciate the lessons it has bestowed upon me, the unexpected blessings, and the opportunities for self-discovery.

I thank my family, who have been my unwavering pillars throughout the years. Their unconditional love, constant support, and ability to motivate me in difficult times have been an invaluable gift. To my parents, for their guidance and example of perseverance. To my sister, for her complicity and deep connection. I appreciate their presence in my life, which has been an endless source of strength and love.

I am grateful to the individuals who have contributed to the creation of this book. To those who have shared their wisdom, experience, and unique perspectives. I thank my colleagues, friends, and mentors, whose voices have enriched my knowledge and challenged my own ideas and beliefs. Their collaboration has been essential in bringing this project to life and sharing its value with others.

I appreciate all the brave and empowered women who have left their mark on the world. Those who have defied norms, overcome obstacles, and left an inspiring legacy. Their stories and achievements remind us of the strength, determination, and unlimited potential that resides within us.

Ultimately, I am thankful to life itself for all the experiences that have allowed me to grow, learn, and discover my own path. Through the ups and downs, moments of joy, and challenges, I have found an inner voice that propels me forward and urges me to pursue fulfillment in all areas of my life.

May this book serve as a source of inspiration and empowerment for all the women who read it. May they find within its pages a reminder of their own power, resilience, and ability to live a fulfilling and satisfying life. Together, we can create a world where all women are free to embrace their authenticity, love without limits, and achieve fulfillment in every aspect of their lives.

To all the brave and passionate women, to my family, to those who have been part of this journey, and to life itself, I thank you from the bottom of my heart. May our voices rise and our lives shine with the strength and beauty that resides within us.

May we live fully, love unconditionally, and embrace our true essence!
With gratitude and love,

Susanna Blumen

ABOUT THE AUTHOR

The author, Susanna Blumen, is an educator of Spanish and German heritage with extensive experience in traveling and immersing herself in different countries and cultures. Throughout her journey, she has collaborated with various non-governmental organizations, focusing on the field of education and personal development.

Passionate about education, philosophy, and personal growth, Susanna has dedicated her career to exploring and sharing knowledge in these areas. Her multicultural experience has provided her with an enriching perspective and a deep understanding of diverse ways of life and thought.

With a focus on empowerment and personal transformation, Susanna seeks to inspire others through her writings, workshops, and talks. Her goal is to help individuals discover their potential, develop a resilient mindset, and find fulfillment in all areas of their lives..

Through her commitment to education and her passion for personal growth, Susanna Blumen has become an inspiring voice for those seeking to achieve a meaningful and fulfilling life.

Made in the USA
Las Vegas, NV
13 January 2024